Waltzing
with
Water

Waltzing with Water

Tempos in Verse

poems by
Elizabeth Spencer Spragins

Shanti Arts Publishing
Brunswick, Maine

Waltzing with Water
Tempos in Verse

Copyright © 2021 Elizabeth Spencer Spragins

All Rights Reserved
This book or any portion thereof may not be reproduced
or used in any manner whatsoever without the
express written permission of the publisher except
for the use of brief quotations in a book review.

Published by Shanti Arts Publishing
Interior and cover design by Shanti Arts Designs

Cover and interior images by C. B. Cote (©)
and used with her permission

Shanti Arts LLC
193 Hillside Road
Brunswick, Maine 04011
shantiarts.com

Printed in the United States of America

ISBN: 978-1-951651-59-6 (softcover)

Library of Congress Control Number: 2020952650

for Lynne, mover of mountains

Contents

Adagio

Emergence	12
Resilience	13
Guardians	14
Cemetery Moss	15
Opening Notes	16
Still Seas	17
Lullaby	18
Jewels of the Night	19
Rainbow Trout	20
Journeys	21
Mist	22
Sun Bathing	23
Drought	24
Mirage	25
On Reflection	26
Tableau on the Shore	27
Somnolence	28
Sea Stars	29
Lost at Sea	30
Erasure	31
La Abuelita (The Grandmother)	32
Supplicants	33
Sand	34
Garden Meditation	35
Fire	36
Casualties	37
Unrest	38
Within Reach	39
Icicle Harps	40
Solstice	41

Andante

Braids	44
The Other Side	45
High Tide	46
Tides	47
Beads	48
Rain Drops	49
Shells	50
Clarity	51
Knots	52
The Brink of Life	53
High Trails	54
Ice Age	55
Luminescence	56
After Hurricane Maria	57
Seams	58

Solace	59
Heaviness	60
Crystal Momentum	61
Ice Sculptures	62
Seas of Snow	63
Winter Prey	64
Wisdom	65

Allegro

Prelude	68
Petals	69
Cascades	70
Equilibrium	71
Before the Flood	72
Torrents	73
Storm Surge	74
Mounted on the Mist	75
Before the Breach	76
Rio Grande Gorge	77
Falls	78
Racing the Day	79
Cloaked	80
Lightning	81
Flash Flood	82
Scorched	83
Firebolts	84
Giant	85
Night Rain	86
Sleep	87
Mustangs	88
Cracks	89
Avalanche	90
Pursuit	91
Pups	92
On Edge	93

Notes	95
Acknowledgements	99
About the Author	101

. . . . Adagio

Emergence

    watersoaked feathers
    wake in alabaster wombs—
    a beak breaks the shell
    and defiant daffodils
    push through crusted sleet and snow

        — Apex, North Carolina

Resilience

unexpected frost
sparkles on the weary wood—
buds on bare branches
swell with promises of pears
in the fragrant April rain

— Fredericksburg, Virginia

Guardians

> cherry tree matrons
> hold bouquets in steady hands
> when soft rain blossoms
> petals wander on the wind
> far from nests and knotted knees
>
> *– Washington, DC*

Cemetery Moss

a brisk morning breeze
wanders quiet corridors—
green velvet carpets
beaded with the dew of dawn
soften sorrows carved in stone

*— Blandford Cemetery,
Petersburg, Virginia*

Opening Notes

drowsy morning mist
rises with the lilt of loons
when a fern uncurls
slender fingers pearled with dew
stroke the strings of hidden harps

— *Damariscotta, Maine*

Still Seas

cerulean skies
glisten in the looking glass—
a sea of bluebells
sweeps across the forest floor
and stones sink into silence

*— Lewis Ginter Botanical
Garden, Richmond, Virginia*

Lullaby

clouds curtain the sun
and spring peepers fall silent
when rain drums softly
on a fish pond stocked with dreams
cattails droop and drift toward sleep

— Marietta, Georgia

Jewels of the Night

water lilies wake
and scent the dusk with secrets
pressed into a pod
petals fold their memories
with laments of lavender

*— Kenilworth Aquatic
Gardens, Washington, DC*

Rainbow Trout

a silent osprey
rows through air on feathered oars—
unrippled waters
hold a rainbow in their hands
and brace for untucked talons

*— Deep Creek Lake,
McHenry, Maryland*

Journeys

> in evergreen shade
> mosses doze upon their beds
> while stepping stones rest
> I sip unhurried waters
> that whisper all will be well
>
> *– Ripton, Vermont*

Mist

a maidenhair fern
lifts her face to morning mist—
the fragrance of rain
walks lightly through this woodland
on slippers laced with diamonds

*— Tongass National
Forest, Alaska*

Sun Bathing

> warm watermelons
> bathe beneath the thirsty sun—
> a sudden shower
> drenches wilted vines and leaves
> that pop up like umbrellas
>
> *– Albany, Georgia*

Drought

afternoon thickens
with heavy heat and thunder—
the first drop of rain
plants a kiss on fevered earth
that thirsts for cool and comfort

*— Chimney Rock,
North Carolina*

Mirage

    a river of rocks
    nestles deeper in its bed
    bereft of water
    skipping stones collect star dust
    and bathe in pools of moonlight

        – Fredericksburg, Virginia

On Reflection

> a silent tree frog
> clings to broken shelves of stone
> rippled by the breeze
> water colors blend and blur
> illusions of perfection
>
> — Fredericksburg, Virginia

Tableau on the Shore

two fawns turn and stare
as my kayak skirts the cove
fiddleheads stand poised
in a bank of lady ferns
and nothing breaks their stillness

— Lake Mooney,
Fredericksburg, Virginia

Somnolence

slender blue fingers
fondle alabaster clouds—
a drowsy river
fluffs the pillows of her bed
and settles into slumber

— Tred Avon River,
Oxford, Maryland

Sea Stars

melodies of moons
linger in a tidal pool
caressed by currents
unsung daughters of the stars
press their palms to silvered sand

– *San Juan, Puerto Rico*

Lost at Sea

a coral garden
blooms among unburied bones—
secretive waters
cradle ghostly galleons
and the bitter dregs of dreams

— San Juan, Puerto Rico

Erasure

a few drops of rain
pummel wrinkles in the earth—
lavender blossoms
in a cleft filled with sagebrush
where scents of bitterness fade

— Santa Fe, New Mexico

La Abuelita (The Grandmother)

> furrows in the field
> watered with a weary hand—
> another wrinkle
> tilled into an autumn face
> harrows hope from fear of frost
>
> — Taos, New Mexico

Supplicants

dessicated stones
part their sun-cracked lips and drink
a pittance of rain
wrung from pockets of the clouds
stirs the dust in earthen urns

*— Desert Botanical Garden,
Phoenix, Arizona*

Sand

as linden leaves drift
over quiet riverbanks
waves lick the sandbar
that holds a pair of footprints
next to crumbled castle walls

*— Rappahannock River,
Fredericksburg, Virginia*

Garden Meditation

    gilded ginkgo leaves
    coast upon the clarity
    between earth and sky
    murmurs I mistake for rain
    pull my gaze from painted ground

*– Lewis Ginter Botanical
Garden, Richmond, Virginia*

Fire

soft blankets of moss
draped across the stoic stones—
a river so cold
cannot quench the crimson leaves
or tapers lit by twilight

— Stockbridge, Massachusetts

Casualties

the last dogwood leaves
dance with twilight tenderness—
a crimson carpet
frays where rocks and rivers meet
memories of those long dead

– Charlottesville, Virginia

Unrest

a fractured rainbow
spans the silence of this loch
where there is no bridge
to the isle where gravestones grow
my longing paints a pathway

*— Eilean Munde,
Glencoe, Scotland*

Within Reach

a single snowflake
tingles on my outstretched palm
so far from my heart
warmth that tunnels through the blood
cracks a weakened wall of ice

– Chicago, Illinois

Icicle Harps

when frozen strings snap
and music melts at morning
the wind holds her harp
against an oaken shoulder
and rests her weary fingers

— *Falmouth, Virginia*

Solstice

    waves of crimson clouds
    breach the banks of winter night—
    an ocean aflame
    cups the dawn in white-gloved hands
    so frigid and so fragile

              — Fish Creek, Wisconsin

. . . . Andante

Braids

April arroyos
weave the waters through burnt sand—
red willow baskets
ripe with roasted piñon nuts
cradle patterns of the past

— Taos, New Mexico

The Other Side

warm waters wander
far beyond my barefoot boy—
ripples from a stone
that sinks into the silence
carry cries that no one hears

> *— Border Crossing Station at*
> *Rio Grande City, Texas*

High Tide

an outgoing wave
tugs at sand beneath bare feet—
arms without anchor
brush tangled ropes of seaweed
tethered to an unmoored moon

*— Sealife Aquarium,
Grapevine, Texas*

Tides

    a seahorse grazes
    in the undulating grass
    caressed by currents
    meadows ripple with lush waves—
    my mare forsakes the shallows

                      – Sealife Aquarium,
                             Grapevine, Texas

Beads

clusters of black pearls
press into the palms of clouds—
a broken necklace
that slips between my fingers
rains upon this garden path

*— Lewis Ginter Botanical
Garden, Richmond, Virginia*

Rain Drops

    two great-tailed grackles
    strut through puddles on my lawn—
    folded umbrellas
    stitched with iridescent beads
    shimmer in the slanted light

        — Fredericksburg, Virginia

Shells

> tides lift my footprints
> from the saturated sand
> where seashells linger
> waves rock their seaweed cradles
> to the rhythm of my heart
>
> — Beaufort, North Carolina

Clarity

cotton clouds adrift
on this liquid looking glass
beneath the mountain
a stately great blue heron
slowly walks across the sky

– Ticonderoga, New York

Knots

sailboats rock gently
as a breeze tugs braided lines
tethered to the pier
my rod strains against a trout
that tacks toward open water

— *Door County, Wisconsin*

The Brink of Life

> the river spirit
> carves her likeness into stone—
> a fluid sculpture
> folds her secrets close to heart
> with the final breath of day

> *— Grand Canyon*
> *Village, Arizona*

High Trails

>as thunder thickens
>storm clouds stalk a fallen sun—
>footprints of the rain
>rest upon unwrinkled roads
>and sink into their softness

>>— Taos, New Mexico

Ice Age

a summer glacier
opens her reluctant hands—
blue sapphires sparkle
in waters that remember
contours of a crystal cage

— Mendenhall Glacier, Alaska

Luminescence

moonstones of blue green
glow in waves of liquid light
when we stir the stars
and dip our oars in wonder
magic dances on my hand

*— Laguna Grande, Fajardo,
Puerto Rico*

After Hurricane Maria

> houses ripped from roots
> rest their wreckage on high hills
> when the coquí sings
> and broken palms reach for rain
> hope falls lightly in my hand
>
> — San Juan, Puerto Rico

Seams

a curtain of rain
stitched between the sea and sky—
blended blue and black
overlay the threads of gold
in unfinished tapestries

*— Fairview Lawn Cemetery,
Halifax, Nova Scotia, Canada*

Solace

a gray wind wanders
past an empty stretch of sand—
two faded footprints
pointed toward an inland road
linger for one moment more

— *Colonial Beach, Virginia*

Heaviness

a sea of snowflakes
rises over rabbit tracks—
the wooden bridge sags
under wet winter blankets
raveled by relentless rain

— *Gettysburg, Pennsylvania*

Crystal Momentum

the winter river
lingers just before she leaps—
frozen water falls
into silent realms of sleep
that fetter time and sorrow

— *Niagara Falls, New York*

Ice Sculptures

    rivulets of green
    nibble crusted ice from snow—
    softness lies beneath
    edges of cold memories
    thawed with time and tender hands

        — Ann Arbor, Michigan

Seas of Snow

the moon sails her skiff
over oceans filled with foam—
waves of combed cotton
glisten on a frozen field
lit by lanterns of the sky

— *Fredericksburg, Virginia*

Winter Prey

gripped by frozen fangs
hemlocks sink to bended knees—
the wolf of winter
slinks into a knife-edged night
as she howls her hunger song

— *Damariscotta, Maine*

Wisdom

a lean winter moon
wanders barefoot at low tide
wrinkles in the sand
of a face with weathered eyes
channel sorrows out to sea

– Beaufort, North Carolina

. . . . Allegro

Prelude

a tune of five notes
skips across the morning fog—
ripples of birdsong
swell with waves that kiss cold sand
and linger for a heartbeat

— Colonial Beach, Virginia

Petals

April wind waltzes
in the flowered arms of trees—
a brook hums softly
while she braids her silver hair
with fallen cherry blossoms

— *Washington, DC*

Cascades

wild roses tumble
over roadside rocks and weeds—
fickle waterfalls
blossom over barren earth
and color pools at daybreak

— *Blue Ridge Parkway,*
Virginia

Equilibrium

> an uneven stone
> leans upon a lifeless limb
> balanced on the bluff
> seedlings of a willow oak
> sink their roots where water falls
>
> *— Great Falls Park,*
> *McLean, Virginia*

Before the Flood

    the river drowses
    under downy cloaks of clouds—
    warning drums of rain
    drown the silence with a dirge
    as water demons waken

*— Cape Fear River,
Fayetteville, North Carolina*

Torrents

when this river roars
the red oak rocks her cradle—
a nest that slumbers
high above the turbulence
holds certainty of swallows

*— Rappahannock River,
Fredericksburg, Virginia*

Storm Surge

    a river of rain
    charges up the battered bank—
    runaway horses
    leap the fence for open fields
    and thunder into freedom

*— Rappahannock River,
Fredericksburg, Virginia*

Mounted on the Mist

>when thunder wakens
>from a sultry summer sleep
>the rain comes riding
>a herd of phantom horses
>and unbraids their misted manes

>*– Charleston, South Carolina*

Before the Breach

    this hungry river
    gnaws the hollow bones of banks—
    knotted cypress knees
    bend beneath the weight of wind
    summoned by a sleepless eye

— Tampa, Florida

Rio Grande Gorge

> drunken waters reel
> from rocky banks to boulders—
> a cauldron of clouds
> simmers as the twilight burns
> incense of an August rain
>
> — Taos, New Mexico

Falls

> rapids roar and buck
> beneath twigs riding bareback
> just before free fall
> I grip rigging of my dreams
> and wrestle fear with one hand
>
> — Laramie, Wyoming

Racing the Day

>   when my vessel leaps
>   and canters through the currents
>   wind song fills my sails
>   with laments of buoy bells—
>   I taste the salt of twilight

>   — Annapolis, Maryland

Cloaked

black curtains billow
just beyond the furrowed fields
encircled by storms
my thoughts thunder with each bolt
that rips the seams of solace

— *Charlottesville, Virginia*

Lightning

a jagged needle
stitches patches to the sky—
uneven hemlines
in tattered cotton curtains
tear beneath the weight of rain

– Seattle, Washington

Flash Flood

> a desert furrow
> boils under sun-scorched skies
> with thickness of blood
> chocolate *con churros*
> burns the dregs of bitterness
>
>   — *Albuquerque, New Mexico*

Scorched

skies of cobalt blue
melt beneath the weight of clouds
heavy with thunder
my words of white-hot fury
cool unspoken in the rain

*— Standing Rock Sioux
Reservation, North Dakota*

Firebolts

> clouds on black chargers
> pour across the battlefield
> pursued by thunder
> lightning leaps across a lake
> and burns the bridge behind him

> *— Taos, New Mexico*

Giant

a lone redwood stands
in this remnant of forest—
my footsteps falter
but I balance on the log
that spans turbulent waters

— Redwood National Park,
California

Night Rain

midnight rain bullets
through this silver-plated pond—
ripples in a glass
mar the mirror of full moon
as her lantern dims and dies

— *Fredericksburg, Virginia*

Sleep

the river thrashes
under white winter blankets
as sheets of ice thin
fingers of the newly drowned
no longer clutch at corners

— Montreal, Québec, Canada

Mustangs

a skittish river
bucks and rolls within its banks
the cold winter rains
on weathered backs of boulders
braced against unbroken seas

— Rio Grande Gorge,
New Mexico

Cracks

gray water gallops
through a fissure filled with dusk–
wrinkles in the rocks
cradle seedlings of a spruce
that no longer lifts her limbs

> *– Great Falls Park,*
> *McLean, Virginia*

Avalanche

the mountain shudders
and rolls a restless shoulder
weary of winter
ice bears unfold rumpled sheets
of the fragile frozen seas

*— Arctic National Wildlife
Refuge, Alaska*

Pursuit

a frozen river
disappears into darkness
following the moon
my sled surges over snow
as dogs lap joy from each mile

— *Fairbanks, Alaska*

Pups

    river otters race
    up a winter water slide—
    untried toboggans
    teeter on the taste of bliss
    over crust of uncut snow

*– Yellowstone National
Park, Wyoming*

On Edge

when day fire dances
to the brink of brittle ice
winter water falls
onto backs of unstacked stones
at rest within the rapids

— *Middlebury Falls,*
Middlebury, Vermont

Notes

"Cemetery Moss"
Blandford Cemetery holds the remains of approximately 30,000 Confederate soldiers who were buried in a mass grave on Memorial Hill.

"Casualties"
More than 22,000 wounded soldiers received treatment at the Charlottesville military hospital during the American Civil War. Over 150 years after that conflict, racial tensions again erupted in violence and bloodshed. The casualties included Heather Heyer, a civil rights activist who was killed when white supremacists attending a "Unite the Right" rally attacked counterprotesters on August 12, 2017.

"Unrest"
Eilean Munde, also known as Graveyard Island, lies near the shore of Loch Leven. For centuries, this uninhabited site has served as a burial ground for the Stewart, Cameron, and MacDonald clans.

"The Brink of Life"
During daylight hours, differences in temperature generate air currents within the Grand Canyon. Local lore holds that at nightfall, when warm air rises and cooler air sinks for the final time, the canyon breathes its "last breath of the day."

"Luminescence"
Laguna Grande is one of three bioluminescent bays in Puerto Rico. The dinoflagellates in these waters glow with an eerie blue-green light when disturbed.

"After Hurricane Maria"
Hurricane Maria struck Puerto Rico on September 20, 2017. One month later, approximately 80% of the island remained without power. The coquí is a frog native to Puerto Rico. The cheerful call of the male is a distinctive feature of evenings on the island.

"Seams"
After RMS Titanic sank on April 15, 1912, the bodies of 121 victims were buried at Fairview Lawn Cemetery in Halifax, Nova Scotia, Canada.

"Falls"
Rigging is the equipment that a bareback rider grips in rodeos.

"Flash Flood"
Churros are fried-dough pastry "sticks" that are traditionally dipped in thick hot chocolate.

"Avalanche"
Ice bears are polar bears.

Acknowledgements

I am deeply grateful to the following journals and anthologies, in which some of these poems first appeared or are forthcoming:

Adelaide Literary Magazine
America 2020
Ariel Chart
Atlas Poetica 28
Bamboo Hut: Journal of Contemporary Tanshi
Black Bough Poetry
Blueline
Bold + Italic Magazine
Borrowed Solace
Dual Coast Magazine
Earth: Our Common Ground: A Song of Short Songs
Ethos Literary Journal
Halcyon Days
Page & Spine
Pangolin Review
Peacock Journal
Red Coyote

Red Wolf Journal
Riverbabble
Rockvale Review
Sin Fronteras/ Writers Without Borders
Skylark: A Tanka Journal
Songs of Eretz Poetry Review
Time of Singing
Yasou! A Celebration of Life

In addition, "Crystal Momentum" and "Seas of Snow" were first published in *With No Bridle for the Breeze: Ungrounded Verse*, by Elizabeth Spencer Spragins. Brunswick, Maine: Shanti Arts Publishing. Print.

"Emergence," "Opening Notes," and "Rainbow Trout" were first published in the microchapbook "Song Feathers." *Origami Poems Project,* June 2020. Web. https://www.origamipoems.com/poets/424-elizabeth-spencer-spragins.

About the Author

Elizabeth Spencer Spragins is a fiber artist, writer, and poet who taught in North Carolina community colleges for more than a decade before returning to her home state of Virginia. Her short fiction, tanka, and bardic verse in the Celtic style have appeared in more than 70 journals and anthologies in nine countries. She is the author of *With No Bridle for the Breeze: Ungrounded Verse* (Shanti Arts Publishing) and *The Language of Bones: American Journeys Through Bardic Verse* (Kelsay Books).

— www.elizabethspencerspragins.wordpress.com

SHANTI ARTS

NATURE · ART · SPIRIT

Please visit us online
to browse our entire book catalog,
including poetry collections and fiction,
books on travel, nature, healing, art,
photography, and more.

Also take a look at our highly
regarded art and literary journal,
Still Point Arts Quarterly, which
may be downloaded for free.

www.shantiarts.com

www.ingramcontent.com/pod-product-compliance
Lightning Source LLC
Chambersburg PA
CBHW070450050426
42451CB00015B/3420